TURKISH COOKING

Gülseren Ramazanoğlu & Margaret Oliphant

A TURIZM YAYINLARI

front cover
Lamb and chicken *şiş kebab*

back cover
Turkish Coffee, *Tarhana* soup, Lamb chops and
Turkish Delight

pictures
Archives of A Turizm Yayınları

editor
Güzin Sancaklı

First printing 1997
Fourth printing 2005

ISBN 975-7199-76-1

Copyright © A Turizm Yayınları

Publishers
A Turizm Yayınları
Şifa Hamamı Sokak 18/2
34122 Sultanahmet, İstanbul, Turkey
Tel: (0212) 516 24 97 Fax: (0212) 516 41 65
info@aturizm.com

CONTENTS

INTRODUCTION

Turkish food is not only delicious, but it is also as interesting and varied as the country itself. Although in general it is neither hot nor very spicy, in the southeast some Arab influence is evident. Food is eaten according to the seasons and freshness is one of the hallmarks of this cuisine. So too is a respect for tradition, with many dishes still being made in the same way as they have been for generations. Although food preparation has been affected by increasing modernisation, this is less evident in Turkish homes than in those of many other countries.

For the most part, Turkish food is not difficult to prepare and as virtually all the ingredients can now be bought in Western countries, it is easy to re-create the flavours of Turkey in your own kitchen.

I must admit to being in love with the country, its people, its culture and of course, its food. But for any person with an interest in food, a visit to Turkey should, if possible, include a walk through the Spice Market in Istanbul or the Food Market in Antalya or any of the countless markets in smaller towns.

In summer there are piles of gleaming red tomatoes and dusky aubergines of all shapes and sizes, and a splendid array of many other vegetables. There is also a seemingly infinite variety of fresh, pungent scented herbs and olives, black, green, golden, plain or stuffed; piles of fresh vineleaves lie waiting to be filled with delicious mixtures of rice, raisins and pine-nuts. In autumn and winter, large and healthy looking root vegetables vie for space with piles of nuts and dried fruits, above which hang chains of dried vegetables, including peppers and okra, both useful additions to winter stews. And then there is the heady, aromatic scent of innumerable spices displayed in great heaps or in open sacks, red paprika, golden turmeric, black and brown cloves and peppers.

If a Turkish market is a treasure store for Foodies, so too is the large stock of recipes available, one of the legacies of the Turks' wide ranging and eventful history.

In the eighth century there were nomadic Turks settled in the Xinjiang province of western China. Having been pushed westward by the Mongols, in the tenth and eleventh centuries, under the leadership of the Selcuk dynasty they established kingdoms in Persia and in Anatolia.

Following the demise of the Selcuks in the thirteenth century, the Ottoman dynasty became the ruling power in Anatolia and in 1453 captured Constantinople from the Byzantines. Turkish hegemony, already extending over Greece and part of the Balkans, later embraced part of Eastern Europe. To the south, the Ottoman empire came to include the Levant, Palestine, Syria, Iraq and Arabia. Egypt and the countries of North Africa, as well as Cyprus, Crete and Malta, also became part or this huge empire. For a time, in the sixteenth century, but for Spain, France and Italy, the Mediterranean was effectively under Ottoman control.

In one way or another, the menu of these once pastoral nomadic people was extended by their contacts with so many different worlds. Nevertheless, some very characteristic Turkish food dates back to the time of their nomadic ancestors; these include various forms of grilled meat, preserved and salted meat known as *pastırma*, and *yoğurt*, or fermented milk. From the Chinese they learnt to cook pasta dishes, including noodles and *mantı*, which is not unlike ravioli. It is possible that the stuffed (*dolma*) and wrapped (*sarma*) vegetable dishes that are such a feature of Turkish cuisine, had their origins in the stuffed pasta dishes prepared since the time of their earlier contacts with the Chinese.

From the Persians the Turks learnt the art or cooking rice and also the use of various fruits and nuts, particularly walnuts and pine nuts, either for sweet dishes such as *hoşaf*, stewed fruits, or as a part of meat dishes.

Sinameki
Thyme

Havlican
Galanda

Yeni Bahar
Allspice

Çam Fıstık
Pine nuts

Zencefil
Ginger

Muskat
Nutmeg

Susam
Sesame

Kırmızı Pul Biber
Chili pepper

Karabiber
Black pepper

Tarçın
Cinnamon

Kekik
Thyme

Kimyon
Cumin

ÇORBALAR
(SOUPS)

*M*any Turkish soups are effectively a meal in their own right, a tradition that goes back to nomadic times. Visitors to the coastal resorts or those who have not been to Turkey, often do not realise that parts of it can get very cold and so the making of hearty and sustaining soups has continued. Although as elsewhere, soup is often served at the beginning of a meal, it is not restricted to any particular time of the day and in rural Anatolia, it is often served at breakfast. There are many types of soup, thin, thick, meat or vegetable and there are special soups for different occasions, such as Wedding soup, with lemon and egg, which is very popular and no longer confined to weddings. Believed to ward off hangovers, tripe soup is sold in special shops which stay open all night to revive the bibulous. Pulses and various grains are widely used and indeed it seems that in Turkey there is little that is edible which that is not used for making soup.

Tarhana Çorbası
(Winter Soup)

SERVES 4

This traditional store cupboard soup, which is based on a powder made from yoghurt, red peppers and tomatoes, is particularly good in cold weather. At the end of summer, in villages and the countryside, one can still see batches of *tarhana* set out to dry. Although many urban Turkish women make their own *tarhana*, nowadays it can also be bought ready prepared. For those unable to buy it, or who prefer to make their own, the instructions are for about 50 servings; quantities can be reduced, but it is easier to knead and prepare a larger amount; it keeps for several months at room temperature and longer in a fridge. *Tarhana* base may sound complicated to make, but it is not; nor is it very time consuming and in an emergency it is far nicer than packaged soup.

2 puddingspoons tarhana powder	salt, pepper
5 drinking glasses stock or dissolved	1 tablespoon melted butter
stock-cube	1/2 teaspoon cayenne or paprika
1 teaglass milk	

The desired thickness depends on personal taste, but as a general guide, use 20 grammes of powder to 1/2 litre liquid.

Mix the powder and milk to a creamy consistency, adding stock gradually; stir frequently to avoid formation of lumps. Bring gradually to the boil, simmer gently for about 15 to 20 minutes and stir regularly; melt butter and add the cayenne or paprika; pour this mixture into the soup and serve. For a more substantial soup, slices of Turkish *sucuk* sausage or any spicy sausage may be added.

Tarhana base

500 grammes flour	1 to 2 large onions (roughly 500
500 grammes tomatoes, finely	grammes weight)
chopped	1 teaspoon red pepper (paprika)
500 grammes red peppers, baked,	Pinch cayenne
skinned, finely chopped	1 teaspoon black pepper
500 grammes yoghurt	1 tablespoon salt

Mix above ingredients together; make a dough as if preparing bread; knead well; place on floured wooden board, cover and stand aside until it rises; knead again. Continue this procedure once a day for about five days. Then divide dough into 3 or 4 pieces, flatten and leave them uncovered to dry outside for 3 or 4 days (in England this is probably best made during a warm dry spell). When dry, pound dough to a powder (this can also be done in a grinder or food blender) and store in jars.

Mısır Çorbası
(Corn Soup)

. . . .

SERVES 4

The warm, wet climate of the Black Sea region provides abundant crops of tobacco, hazelnuts, tea, cherries and corn. In this part of Turkey, cornflour is used extensively in cooking. If one has tins of corn in the store cupboard, this useful emergency soup is a modern adaptation of more substantial corn based dishes.

1 large tin corn — unsweetened is
* better*
1 onion
¹/₂ tablespoon butter
3 glasses chicken stock or dissolved

* stock-cube*
¹/₄ bunch parsley - optional
¹/₂ glass cream or milk
salt
black pepper

Soften onion in butter; add the corn and stock and heat gently. If using stock-cube, warm corn and then pour on the hot stock. When corn is softened, keep back a small quantity of corn to garnish and place mixture in blender, to which is added a little cream or milk. Blend to creamy consistency. Adjust seasoning and sprinkle with parsley and corn. A little yoghurt may be added when serving.

Ezo Gelin Çorbası
(Lentil and *Bulgur* Soup)

SERVES 4 TO 6

In this sustaining soup, which is very good in winter, lentils are combined with *bulgur*, cracked wheat (husked and pounded wheat). Ever since the nomadic Turks began to settle and grow crops, such as wheat, barley and millet, bulgur has been part of the Turkish diet.

100 grammes red lentils
1 ¼ litres beef or chicken stock or dissolved stock cube
1 onion, chopped
30 grammes bulgur
1 tablespoon butter
1 tablespoon tomato purée

pinch allspice or mace
2 teaspoons dried mint
salt
black pepper
a few fresh mint leaves, chopped, to garnish

Soften onion in butter; add lentils, *bulgur*, tomato purée, stock, 1 teaspoon mint, allspice, salt and pepper. Cook on a low heat, stirring from time to time, until tender and the soup has reached the consistency of cream. Add the remaining mint and simmer for a few minutes. Adjust seasoning, sprinkle with chopped fresh mint.

Mercimek Çorbası
(Lentil Soup)

● ●

SERVES 4

1 large chopped onion
1 or 2 carrots
1 medium to large potato
1 glass red lentils
6 glasses chicken stock or dissolved
  stock-cube
large nut of butter
¼ glass milk or single cream
salt, pepper to season (reduce salt if
  stock-cube used)

5 to 6 sprigs fresh mint or ½
  tablesoon dried mint.
OR ALTERNATIVELY for soup with
  cumin: replace mint with 1½ to 2
  puddingspoons ground cumin
2 tablespoons melted butter,
for a delicious and spicy lentil soup
  nearly sizzling ½ teaspoon
  paprika to stir into the hot butter
croutons

Place onion, carrots and potato in butter; cook over gentle heat until they start to soften. Add lentils, stock, seasoning and mint (or cumin). Cook either in a pressure cooker for about 15 minutes or over a low heat, stirring from time to time. When soft, add milk or cream and blend in food blender. Season to taste and return to heat to simmer for a few minutes. Serve with appropriate garnish.

NOTE: green or brown lentils could be used, in which case approximately one glass extra stock is necessary.

Yayla Çorbası
(Yoghurt and Mint Soup)

SERVES 4

Ever since the Turks' nomadic ancestors in Central Asia first made *yoğurt* it has formed an important part of the Turkish diet. *Yayla* means both an upland pasture and by extension, a summer residence, which would originally have been in the highlands, but also came to mean a summer retreat. This very traditional soup is both delicious and easy to make.

3 drinking glasses of water
1 teaspoon salt
1 to 2 tablespoons rice, depending
  on taste

500 grammes yoghurt
1 extra drinking glass of water
1 puddingspoon dried mint
1 tablespoon melted butter

Bring the first three ingredients to the boil in a good sized saucepan. Meanwhile, combine the yoghurt and extra glass of water to make *ayran*, mixing well with a fork. Pour a little of the rice and water mixture onto the *ayran* and mix, before adding the ayran to the saucepan. Add the mint, reserving a little; stir well and let simmer until creamy, about 15 to 20 minutes. Finally, add the melted butter and the balance of the mint and stir for a minute or so.

Sprinkle with mint to serve.

Düğün Çorbası
(Wedding Soup)

SERVES 4

2 tablespoons rice flour - ordinary
   flour could also be used
1 egg
juice of ½ lemon
1 glass water
3 glasses stock from bone with
   some meat on
OR same quantity meat stock cube
shredded cooked meat from stock
   bone

OR 200 grammes finely minced veal
   or lamb, seasoned
1 teaspoon salt — reduce if stock-
   cube used
¼ teaspoon pepper
2 tablespoons melted butter
1 teaspoon red pepper
½ bunch chopped dill to garnish -
   optional

Mix together flour, egg, lemon juice and water; to this mixture carefully add warm stock, stirring all the time to prevent curdling. Add salt and slowly bring nearly to the boil and simmer, stirring regularly. After about 15 to 20 minutes, throw in shredded meat or small pinches of the seasoned mince. Just before serving, melt butter till nearly sizzling and stir in red pepper; add to soup or serve separately. If desired, garnish with chopped dill.

Domates Çorbası
(Tomato Soup)

• •

SERVES 4

Sun ripened tomatoes make a delicious soup, that is quick and easy to prepare. If plenty of tomatoes are available, the quantity can be increased and there is then no need for purée.

750 grammes tomatoes, skinned and chopped
1 onion, finely chopped
½ bunch parsley, finely chopped
¼ teaspoon dried oregano - optional approx. 1 tablespoon butter
2 heaps of teaspoons flour
2 tablespoons tomato purée
3 glasses chicken stock or stock-cube
½ to 1 glass water
pinch of sugar
salt
black pepper
for garnish
grated hard cheese, mature kaşar peynir, but gruyére, or cheddar are fine too.

Soften onion in butter then sprinkle on the flour and blend to coat the onions and cook a little longer to break down the starch, but do not allow to turn colour. Add tomatoes, a pinch of sugar, half of the parsley and stir well. Turn and cook over gentle heat until beginning to soften, but do not allow lumps to form. Slowly add stock, about half of the water, tomato purée, salt, pepper and oregano. Slowly bring to the boil, lower heat, cook gently, uncovered, if necessary adding a little water.

İşkembe Çorbası
(Tripe Soup)

SERVES 6

As this soup is thought to help prevent hangovers, special restaurants serving it, called *işkembeci*, can be found open all night.

1 tripe (sheep), approx.
water for boiling tripe,
bay leaf and pinch mixed herbs
3 soupspoons butter
2 soupspoons flour
2 eggs or 4 yolks of egg
juice of 1 ¹/₂ lemons

1 teaspoon red pepper (paprika)

Sauce to accompany soup
nut of butter
2 tablespoons vinegar
3 cloves garlic, crushed
¹/₂ to 1 tablespoon water

To prepare the tripe: clean and wash it very thoroughly; place it in a large saucepan and cook in the water, uncovered, until boiling. Regularly skim off the foam until there is none left. Only after this, cover and simmer until tender, probably about two hours or in a pressure cooker, one hour. When the tripe is tender, remove and cut it into small pieces and return to the stock; now add the chopped bay leaf, mixed herbs, salt and pepper. Bring back to boil and simmer for a further two hours (or one in pressure cooker), adding water if necessary. When second cooking is done, remove the bay leaf. Then melt two spoons of the butter, add the flour and make a roux, cooking for a few minutes, stirring all the time. Add some of the tripe stock to the roux, stirring well and then pour this mixture into the stock and tripe, blend and cook over a low heat, for about 15 to 20 minutes, stirring regularly and then remove from the heat. Beat the eggs or yolks in a bowl and add the lemon juice. Blend in a little of the soup mixture and then add this sauce very slowly to the soup, stirring constantly until it is all incorporated. Melt the nut of butter in a very small pan and quickly turn the crushed garlic; this is not to be cooked, but merely softened slightly; then remove from heat and stir in vinegar and water; the garlic may simply be mixed with the vinegar, in which case no water need be added, but the slight warming improves the flavour. Pour this sauce into a sauce-dish for serving at the table. Now melt the remaining butter, add the red pepper (paprika) and stir. Adjust the seasoning of the soup and pour the red pepper (paprika) butter over it before serving.

MEZELER VE SALATALAR (MEZES AND SALAD)

*M*ezes are the small dishes of infinite variety both cold and hot, served either at the beginning of the meal as an appetizer or *hors d'oeuvre* or sometimes, even as an entire meal. Foods served at the *meze* table range from slices of melon, white cheese, olives, and simple dishes such as yoghurt with cucumber to the more elaborate, including stuffed mussels, shredded chicken in walnut sauce and hot savoury pastries. Ideally *meze* should be accompanied by rakı, the potent alcoholic drink, flavoured with aniseed, served with ice and water.

Cacık
(Yoghurt and Cucumber Salad)

SERVES 4 TO 6

750 grammes yoghurt
3 large cucumbers, peeled and finely
  chopped
2 cloves garlic, crushed
2 tablespoons fresh mint, finely
  chopped
OR 1 tablespoon dried mint, placed
  in a little warm water, use when

  cooled
4 tablespoons dill - optional
2 spring onions, very finely chopped
  - optional
3 tablespoons olive oil
salt
black pepper

Place cucumbers in sieve and sprinkle with a little salt; leave for about 10 to 15 minutes; squeeze lightly and place in bowl. This process softens the cucumber and some prefer it this way, but it can be eliminated if one is in a hurry. Place the cucumbers in a bowl with the garlic and then beat the yoghurt and a little salt together; when creamy, stir into the cucumbers and add the mint, dill, onion, pepper and if required, a little more salt. Trickle the olive oil on top and chill. Serve with pide or bread.

In Turkey, where the yoghurt is usually thick and creamy, a little water is usually added.

Çoban Salatası
(Shepherd's Salad)

SERVES 4

2 tomatoes, chopped
2 cucumbers, peeled and chopped
2 green peppers (capsicum), seeded
   and chopped
2 spring onions, finely sliced
1 onion, sliced
½ bunch parsley, chopped

6 radishes, sliced
3 to 4 tablespoons olive or sunflower
   oil
juice of 1 to 1 ½ lemons
salt
pepper

Place all the chopped and sliced vegetables and the parsley together in a bowl and mix well. Make a dressing from the oil, lemon juice, salt and pepper. Shortly before serving, add the dressing to the salad.

Çerkez Tavuğu
(Circassian Chicken)

. . . .

SERVES 4 TO 6

This popular dish, as the name indicates, was reputedly acquired from the Circassians.

500 grammes cold chicken, cut in strips
200 grammes walnuts, ground
2 slices white bread
1 tablespoon finely chopped onion
1 clove garlic, crushed

125 ml. chicken stock
1 tablespoon walnut oil
1 ½ teaspoons paprika
salt
pepper

Remove crusts and soak bread in water, then squeeze dry and combine with the walnuts, onion, garlic, half the paprika and the pepper and mix in a blender. Then add chicken stock and mix again until creamy. Place chicken on dish, pour on the sauce, dribble with walnut oil and sprinkle with paprika.

Fava
(Broad Beans Purée)

. . . .

SERVES ABOUT 10

A popular and tasty *meze*, which is very easy to make.

750 grammes dried broad beans, soaked overnight
3 onions, roughly chopped
2 potatoes, peeled and chopped
4 glasses water

1 glass olive oil (250 ml)
½ bunch dill, finely chopped
2 tablespoons sugar
2 teaspoons salt

Rinse and drain the beans. Place in a large saucepan or pressure cooker with all the other ingredients, cover and cook over medium heat; stir occasionaly until beans tender and the liquid has been absorbed. In the pressure cooker this is about half an hour, however, as water may need to be added, the mixture can be partially cooked in pressure cooker to save time and then more slowly finished to be able to adjust if necessary. When thick and all cooked, mash or put in blender; the resulting mixture should be rather like mashed potato of a thick pouring consistency; pour into a shallow serving dish and place to cool. Once cool it can be covered and put in the fridge. Either turn out or cut into individual pieces of diamond or other shapes. Serve cold with a little lemon, olive and dill sprinkled on top.

Ispanak Kökü Salatası
(Spinach Root Salad)

SERVES 4 TO 6

For those who are unable to get spinach roots, the thick stems of the spinach base or chard or similar green vegetables can be substituted.

1 kilo. spinach roots
75 ml. olive oil
3 to 4 tablespoons lemon juice
1/2 teaspoon mustard

pinch of thyme
1/2 teaspoon paprika
salt
freshly ground black pepper

Cut into regular sized lengths; boil in salted water, drain. While still warm, add dressing of oil, lemon juice, mustard, thyme, salt and pepper, but reserve a little to add pour over when cold and then sprinkle with paprika and a little freshly ground pepper.

Gavurdağı Salatası
(Grilled Vegetable Salad)

• •

Named after a mountain near Gaziantep in the south east, where the food is more spicy, this salad is made from vegetables that have been grilled; perhaps in homage to the rocks on the mountain, it includes walnuts. Quantities are not given, as this is a salad to use up vegetables and some ready made ingredients, such as pepperonata can be added.

Use any vegetables suitable for
   grilling:

*the precise proportions do not
   matter; use what is available;
   brushed with oil and sprinkled with
   sumak, salt and black pepper*
courgettes, sliced
peppers, sweet or hot, sliced
thinly sliced carrots

onions
a few whole garlic cloves
tomatoes
mushrooms
sliced aubergine
walnuts, chopped
parsley, chopped
salad dressing
pinch of cayenne

When the vegetables have been grilled and are cold, cut into small pieces; place in bowl with nuts, parsley and turn in dressing.

Humus
(Purée of Chickpeas)

SERVES 4

Although this can now be bought in many food shops and supermarkets, it is simple to make and tastes far better than most ready-made versions.

250 grammes chickpeas
1 ³/₄ to 2 litres water
120 ml olive oil
¹/₂ glass sesame seed paste (tahin)
OR if sesame seed oil available,
* reduce the olive oil to about 50 ml*
* and use 100 ml sesame seed oil;*
* but the precise quantities depend*
* on desired consistency*
3 tablespoons lemon juice
3 cloves garlic, crushed
¹/₂ to 1 teaspoon cayenne
OR paprika if preferred
salt
black pepper
pide

Soak the chickpeas in water overnight; it is better if the water is first heated. Wash and strain; then boil them in salted water until soft. Strain and mash or blend in food processor. Keep back some of the olive oil to adjust consistency if necessary, but add most of it to the purée, together with *tahin*, lemon juice, garlic, cayenne or paprika, salt and pepper and blend until reaching a creamy consistency of desired thickness. Turn onto serving dish, sprinkle with paprika or cayenne and dribble a little oil on top.

Patates Salatası
(Potato Salad)

SERVES 4

500 grammes new potatoes of
    even size
3 spring onions
1 large cucumber — optional
5 tablespoons olive oil
2 tablespoons white wine vinegar

a little mustard
parsley
dill
salt
freshly ground black pepper
paprika

Boil potatoes in skins and remove when cooked, but still firm, then peel and slice. Keep back one spoon of olive oil and make a dressing using the rest of it, the vinegar, mustard, salt and pepper; pour this on the still warm potatoes, turning to coat all the slices. Chop onions finely and slice the cucumber. When the potatoes have cooled, arrange with the cucumbers on a dish on which half the parsley, dill and onions have been scattered and then sprinkle the rest on top, dribble the olive oil and dust with paprika.

Patlıcan Salatası
(Aubergine Purée)

SERVES 4

6 medium aubergines
4 cloves garlic, crushed
120 ml olive oil

juice of 1 lemon
$1/2$ to 1 teaspoon salt

NOTE: precise quantities are not important, the idea is to have a soft purée that has as much or as little garlic or lemon for your taste.

Prick the aubergines with fork; either grill on charcoal or over open flame, turning occasionally until skin is charred and flesh soft; they can be baked in the oven, but the flavour is not as good. When cool enough to handle, but not cold, cut lengthways in half, scoop out the flesh and place in bowl. Mash with fork, add lemon juice, garlic, olive oil and salt; continue mashing until puréed. Place on serving dish.

Sarmısaklı Yoğurtlu Patlıcan Salatası
(Garlic Yoghurt Aubergine Salad/Purée)

SERVES 4

The addition of yoghurt into which garlic has been beaten, turns this into garlic yoghurt aubergine salad/purée. Use between 250 and 500 grammes yoghurt with one or two cloves of crushed garlic or more, depending on taste.

Sirkeli Patlıcan Salatası
(Aubergine Salad with Vinegar)

SERVES 4

1 large aubergine, cubed
3 to 4 spring onions, sliced
4 cloves garlic, crushed
$1/4$ bunch parsley, chopped
1 tablespoon vinegar

1 tablespoon lemon juice
olive oil for frying
salt
pepper

Soak aubergine in salted water for about 15 minutes, rinse and dry well. Fry cubes in olive oil until golden. Drain on kitchen paper; place in bowl, add garlic, spring onions, parsley, vinegar, lemon juice, salt and pepper, and turn lightly.

Haydari
(Yoghurt and Cheese Spread)

SERVES 6

500 grammes yoghurt
125 grammes crumbled white
  cheese
1 to 2 tablespoons olive oil
1 puddingspoon dried mint,

pounded
a little fresh mint, chopped
1 teaspoon paprika
1 teaspoon cayenne
salt

Line a sieve with cheese-cloth; then place in yoghurt in sieve to drain for about an hour. Then beat yoghurt until smooth, working in the mint, paprika, cayenne and cheese and salt if necessary. Put in bowl to chill for a few hours. Before serving, sprnikle with chopped mint and dribble olive oil over surface.

Ezme
(Spicy Tomato and Onion Salad)

. . . .

SERVES 4

This piquant and spicy dish, neither quite
salad nor relish, but something between the
two, can be served as a *meze* or with grilled
meat. The name comes not from the ingredients, but from the texture; in Turkish, *ezme*
means 'puréed' or 'mashed'. It is most easi-
ly made in a food processor.

2 large ripe tomatoes, skinned
1 green pepper, seeds removed
1 small cucumber, peeled and seeds
   removed
2 onions
1 clove garlic, crushed
a few leaves fresh mint
OR $1/4$ teaspoon dried mint
$1/4$ bunch parsley, chopped
1 tablespoon olive oil
1 tablespoon vinegar (though not traditionally
   Turkish, equal parts basilico and wine
   vinegar work well)
$1/2$ teaspoon paprika
$1/4$ teaspoon cayenne - optional
$1/2$ teaspoon salt
$1/2$ teaspoon black pepper

Chop tomatoes, onions, pepper and cucumber in food processor, or chop very finely. If using processor, now add most of the
parsley and the garlic and quickly blend
again. Alternatively, chop the parsley very
finely and make sure the garlic is finely
crushed before adding them. Then turn this
mixture into a sieve to drain excess liquid.
When it has reached a firm consistency, put
it in a bowl, add all the other ingredients and
mix very well. Place in serving dish and flatten with the back of a fork. Leave for a few
hours for the flavour to intensify.

YUMURTALAR
(EGGS)

Ispanaklı Yumurta
(Eggs with Spinach)

....

SERVES 4

*1.5 kilos fresh spinach OR frozen
    spinach for 4
Water to cover spinach
4 eggs
1 onion, chopped
2 cloves garlic, crushed*

*3 to 4 tablespoons butter (depends
    on pan used, non-stick requires
    only 3)
1 ½ teaspoons nutmeg
salt
black pepper*

Prepare spinach: if fresh, wash well, remove any tough stems and cover with boiling water and about 1 ½ teaspoons salt. Cook till tender, about 5 minutes. Drain well and then chop. If frozen, follow instructions depending on whether leaf or chopped. Melt butter, soften onions and garlic and then add spinach; after a few minutes add a pinch of salt, black pepper and nutmeg. Flatten spinach with fork or back of spoon and make four hollows; crack and egg into each and then cover pan, lower heat and cook until the whites have set; the yolks should be soft, but with opaque covering. Slide onto platter or serve individually, with a little sprinkling of black pepper.

Menemen
(Eggs with Tomatoes and Green Peppers)

....

SERVES 4

A delicious combination of flavours, this is a good and quickly made lunch or light supper dish.

*8 eggs
2 medium tomatoes, chopped
1 large green pepper, seeded and
    chopped
2 spring onions, finely sliced
100 grammes white cheese (feta*

*type), crumbled
½ bunch parsley, chopped
2 tablespoons butter
salt
black pepper*

Beat the eggs in a bowl with a little salt and pepper. Melt the butter in a pan, add the onions, tomatoes and pepper and cook until soft. Then pour on the beaten egg and stir lightly for a little, before adding the cheese. Cook, whilst stirring, until just beginning to firm, but still slightly runny and then add the parsley and stir. It should have finished cooking at this point, but if not briefly return to heat until firm but not dry, although individual tastes vary. Season and serve.

Çılbır
(Egg with Yoghurt Sauce)

• •

SERVES 4

This traditional dish makes an unusual lunch or light supper dish. It is basically poached eggs with a yoghurt sauce.

8 eggs
water
1 pudding spoon vinegar
8 tablespoons yoghurt

2 cloves garlic, crushed
2 tablespoons butter
1 teaspoon paprika

Prepare the yoghurt sauce by mixing the garlic into the yoghurt. Stand in a basin of warm water to make tepid. Poach the eggs in water to which the vinegar has been added — this prevents the eggs from spreading too much. Melt the butter in a small pan and stir in the paprika. Slide the eggs onto plates. Pour the yoghurt over and the paprika butter on top of that; season and serve quickly.

Pastırmalı Yumurta
(Eggs with Pastırma)

SERVES 4

Pastırma, a spicy, dried meat, is one of the most ancient kinds of Turkish foods, first made by the nomadic Turks in Central Asia to preserve meat. It is dried, salted, pressed and cured with a paste that consists mainly of red pepper, garlic and fenugreek seeds.

200 grammes pastırma
4 eggs
1 onion, finely chopped
1 glass water

1/3 glass meat stock
1 tablespoon butter
salt
black pepper

Soften the onions in butter and meanwhile remove paste from slices of *pastırma* and place in a separate pan with the water; simmer for a few minutes, then drain. Sprinkle salt and pepper on onions and lay *pastırma* slices over them; pour the warm stock over and then crack in the eggs, to poach; cover and cook until set.

ZEYTİNYAĞLILAR
(OLIVE OIL DISHES)

İmam Bayıldı
(Aubergines with Tomatoes and Onions)

SERVES 4

This dish, one of Turkey's best known, is equally famous for its taste and its name, meaning *imam* fainted; either from delight or because of the cost of the vast quantity of olive oil required to cook it. It is rightly famous and not difficult to make.

4 aubergines of equal size
2 onions, sliced
3 tomatoes, skinned and finely
  chopped
6 cloves of garlic, chopped
1/2 bunch parsley

3/4 glass olive oil
3/4 glass water
juice of half a lemon
1 puddingspoon sugar
1 level teaspoon salt

Cut the stems off aubergines; peeling lengthways, remove skin in alternate strips; then slit lengthways, leaving both ends uncut. Place aubergines in a large bowl of water with one teaspoon salt and leave for half an hour; then drain, dry well. Arrange aubergines next to each other in a large shallow pan and set aside. Very lightly partially soften onions in a little of the olive oil, then add tomatoes, garlic, parsley, sugar and salt; stir, do not cook, but mix together well, remove from heat and stuff mixture into the aubergines. Pour the remaining olive oil, the water and lemon juice over, cover and cook over medium heat for 45 minutes to an hour, until aubergines tender. Leave to cool before carefully transferring to dish. Serve cold as first course.

Zeytinyağlı Taze Fasulye
(Green Beans in Olive Oil)

SERVES 4

The wide range and excellent quality of Turkish vegetables has given this cuisine a great variety of vegetable dishes, often cooked in olive oil and served as a first course either cold or warm, with main dish.

750 grammes stringed or sliced
  green beans (any variety)
1 large or 2 small onions, finely
  chopped
1 large tomato, sliced
1/3 glass of olive oil

3 glasses of water
dash of sugar
pinch of basil or a few fresh leaves
1/2 teaspoon tomato purée - optional
1/2 teaspoon salt
1/4 teaspoon pepper

Gently warm the oil and add all ingredients except water, tomato purée and basil. Stir and cook at high heat until all covered with oil and just about beginning to soften. Then add water which has been brought to the boil, tomato purée and basil. Leave uncovered and cook until vegetables are soft and the water has evaporated. Serve hot or cold with a dribble of olive oil on top. Lemon juice may also be added if eaten cold.

Zeytinyağlı Yaprak / Lahana Dolması
(Stuffed Vine / Cabbage Leaves in Olive Oil)

SERVES 10 OF EITHER

These delicious little parcels are not difficult to make and bear little resemblance in taste to the mass produced variety, which are best avoided. The same stuffing is used for either type and both are eaten cold.

Stuffing for Vine or Cabbage Leaves

250 grammes long grain rice
6 onions, very finely chopped/grated
1 tomato, skinned and finely
  chopped
4 tablespoons pine nuts
2 tablespoons currants
1/2 bunch dill, finely chopped
1/4 bunch fresh mint chopped

1 teaspoon allspice
1/2 teaspoon cinnamon
1 teaspoon sugar
salt
pepper
1 glass olive oil
1 glass hot water

Finely chop or grate onions (or use food processor); using large pan, heat olive oil, fry onions and pine nuts until lightly browned. Add rice, stir and cook for a few minutes; add tomatoes, currants, spices, sugar, water, salt and pepper; stir, cover and cook gently over low heat for about 20 minutes, until liquid is absorbed. Stir in mint and dill and leave to cool.

To Prepare Stuffed Vine Leaves

500 grammes vine leaves (drained
  weight)

Fresh:

*Wash well, place in plenty of boiling
  water for about 2 minutes; quickly
  drain and plunge into cold water;
  remove stalks.*

Preserved in brine:

*Soak overnight or for several hours
  in cold water, rinse well and drain*
400 ml. hot water
100 ml. olive oil
1/4 teaspoon sugar
1 lemon, peeled and sliced

Lay the leaves with glossy side down, matted side up and with the stem towards you (trim if not less than about 1/4 inch). Place a teaspoon of stuffing near the stem end and fold the leaf edges inward over the stuffing, then roll the leaf away from you to form the dolma, which should be finger shaped and a firm little roll. When all ready, tear discarded leaves and line base of large pan. Place the dolma on the bed of leaves, with thir edges downwards and next to each other and make a second layer if necessary. Pour on olive oil, hot water, sugar and arrange the lemon slices on top. Use heatproof plate as a weight, cover, bring to boil, then cook gently for about 35 minutes; when tender, pour off any excess water and leave to cool, with lid on. Serve with lemon wedges.

To Prepare Stuffed Cabbage Leaves

1 large cabbage (loose leafed)
400 ml. hot water
100 ml. olive oil

¼ teaspoon salt
¼ teaspoon sugar
1 lemon, peeled and sliced.

Discard outer leaves to line base of large pan; cut in half, cut away hard core, separate leaves and wash. Boil in salted water till tender; remove carefully (use strainer spoon) and leave to cool. Cut away thick veins, divide leaves into pieces of hand size. Place ball of stuffing at leaf base, fold over edges and roll away from you to make a finger sized *dolma*. Lay with edges down on bed of leaves in pan, add sugar, salt, water, olive oil and arrange lemon slices on top. Weight down with heatproof plate, cover and cook on medium for about 25 minutes. Drain excess liquid and cool with lid on.

Zeytinyağlı Pırasa
(Leeks in Olive Oil)

SERVES 4

750 grammes leeks, washed, sliced
1 carrot, sliced to roughly same size
  as leeks
1 puddingspoon of rice
1/2 bunch parsley, finely chopped

3 tablespoons olive oil
1 1/2 glasses water
1/2 teaspoon salt
1/4 teaspoon pepper

Warm oil in pan, then add all ingredients except water and half the parsley. Cook at high heat, turning regularly until all covered with oil and beginning to soften. Cover with water and cook until soft. Serve hot or cold. If eaten cold, lemon juice may be added.

Zeytinyağlı Taze Bakla
(Fresh Broad Beans in Olive Oil)
∙∙∙

SERVES 4 TO 6

750 grammes fresh broad beans
6 spring onions, sliced
1 onion, chopped
450 ml. water
100 ml. olive oil
60 ml. lemon juice
1 ½ tablespoons flour
1 tablespoon sugar

½ bunch dill
salt
ground black pepper

sauce

400 grammes yoghurt
1 clove garlic, crushed

Wash the beans, rub with salt to remove down, rinse well; top, tail and string; place in bowl in which water, lemon juice and flour have been mixed. Heat a little of the oil and lightly cook the onion, then add spring onions and cook for a minute. Remove, add remaining oil and then the beans and water, flour and lemon mixture, sugar and salt. Bring to the boil, cover and cook an medium heat until tender and some liquid remains. Stir in half the dill and leave to cool. Transfer to serving dish, dribble a little olive oil, sprinkle with dill and freshly ground black pepper. Beat yoghurt with the garlic and serve as accompanying sauce.

SEBZELER
(VEGETABLES)

*A*s a large country with a great range of climate and terrain, Turkey is blessed with an immense variety of vegetables. They are prepared in many different ways, from simple salads to those stewed in olive oil, on their own, in a mixture, or stuffed, to be eaten hot or cold. Some are eaten as part of a course, or at the start of the meal or as part of a *meze* table.

Etli Biber Dolma
(Green Peppers Stuffed with Meat)

. . . .

SERVES 4 TO 6

Many vegetables are stuffed and cooked, either with or without meat in the stuffing. Those with meat are called *etli dolma*, meaning stuffed with meat, and are eaten hot, as a main course, often served with yoghurt and salad. The stuffing in this recipe can be varied by adding raisins, pine nuts, dill or cumin and be used for other vegetables, such as tomatoes, courgettes and aubergines, or to fill cabbage and vine leaves.

6 large sweet green peppers
450 grammes minced lamb or beef
100 grammes uncooked rice
1/2 bunch parsley, finely chopped
2 onions, chopped
2 cloves garlic, crushed
2 tablespoons tomato purée

1 teaspoon allspice
1/2 teaspoon oregano
1 teaspoon salt
1 teaspoon pepper
a few lettuce or vine leaves
water

Slice the tops off the peppers and scoop out the pips. To prepare the stuffing: mix together meat, rice, onions, garlic, 1 spoon tomato purée, parsley, allspice, oregano, salt and pepper. Then stuff into the peppers and replace their tops. Line the bottom of a pot with the leaves and stand the peppers on the leaves; dissolve the second spoon of tomato purée in sufficient water to cover the bottom half of the peppers. After adding the water, cover and simmer over a low heat till cooked, about 40 minutes. They may be baked in a medium oven instead, about 1 hour.

Kabak Dolması
(Courgettes Stuffed with Meat)

. . . .

SERVES 4 TO 6

This stuffing can be used for other vegetables, but goes particularly well with courgettes, though it could be adapted for various squashes and marrow. It is the basic meat stuffing for vegetables with dried chickpeas replacing the rice and dill added.

12 large courgettes
meat stuffing, with following
  changes: replace rice with 100
  grammes white chickpeas replace
  oregano with 1/2 bunch dill, finely
  chopped
3 large tomatoes, skinned and very
  finely chopped

2 glasses hot water
2 tablespoons butter
1/2 bunch dill, chopped
750 grammes yoghurt
pinch sugar
salt
pepper

Wash courgettes, cut off stem ends, scrape with fork and scoop out insides; save the pulp. Stuff with the meat mixture and then place side by side, upright in pan; a small piece of tomato, with skin can be used as a lid for each courgette. Melt the butter in a small pan, add the tomatoes, sugar, salt and pepper and cook gently until it is a thick pulp; add this and the water to the pan with courgettes. Place a heatproof plate as a weight, on top of the courgettes, bring to the boil, cover and cook over low heat for about 45 minutes, or until tender.

Karnıyarık
(Aubergines Stuffed with Minced Meat)

SERVES 4

Turkish cuisine is rich in recipes for aubergine and this one, served with rice and salad, is particularly good.

4 aubergines
olive oil to cover bottom of pan

For the filling:
250 grammes minced veal or lamb; beef can be used but have all the fat trimmed off and have it minced twice.
1 puddingspoon melted butter

1 onion, grated
1/2 bunch parsley finely chopped
1 1/2 teaspoons salt
1/2 teaspoon pepper
1 large tomato, skinned and finely chopped

To garnish:
large tomato sliced in 4
4 thin green peppers

Soften onion in butter; add meat and brown; stir in all other stuffing ingredients and cook uncovered. Meanwhile, peel 4 thin segments lengthwise of the aubergines and then slit the middle, making sure that the slit does not extend to the ends. Turn the aubergines in oil until partly softened and put aside. Then stuff the aubergines with the meat filling. Place a slice of tomato and a pepper on top of each aubergine and bake in moderate oven for about 20 minutes.

Etli Bamya
(Braised Meat with Okra)

• •

SERVES 4 TO 6

Okra is not widely used in Western cooking, but has been a popular vegetable in Turkey since Ottoman times. Here it can be cooked with either lamb or beef.

*500 grammes lamb or beef, cut in
    small cubes
500 grammes fresh okra. trimmed
1 onion, very finely chopped
4 tablespoons butter
3 tomatoes, skinned and chopped
1 glass meat stock*

*1 glass water
1 puddingspoon tomato purée
juice of 1 lemon
1/2 teaspoon thyme
salt
pepper*

Place the okra in a bowl with the water and juice of half the lemon and set aside. Melt the butter and soften the onions; add the meat and brown. Then add the tomatoes, thyme, salt and pepper and cook for a few more minutes, before adding warmed stock. Cook over a low heat for about 20 minutes. Drain the okra, then add it juice of the other half of lemon. Cook gently for about half an hour. Adjust seasoning and serve hot with rice.

Tavuklu Türlü
(Chicken and Vegetable Stew)

. . . .

SERVES 4 TO 6

The addition of okra and aubergine gives this chicken stew a good thick texture and rich flavour without the need for any thickening ingredients.

750 grammes chicken, jointed (or
    drumsticks etc.)
2 onions, chopped
2 cloves garlic, crushed
4 large tomatoes, skinned and
    chopped
2 sweet green peppers, seeded and
    chopped
3 aubergines, peeled and thickly
    sliced
3 courgettes, thickly sliced
250 grammes okra, trimmed
225 grammes green beans, large

slices
2 potatoes, peeled and chopped
150 grammes peas (frozen or fresh)
4 glasses chicken stock (have some
    extra to hand)
1/2 glass water
juice of 1/2 lemon
1 tablespoon tomato purée
4 tablespoons butter
1 bunch parsley, chopped
1 teaspoon thyme or mixed herbs
salt
pepper

Place the okra in a bowl with water and lemon juice. Using a large casserole suitable for oven and electric or gas ring, sauté the chicken pieces in two thirds of the butter, then add onions and garlic and cook together for about 10 minutes; add the tomatoes, potatoes, aubergines, beans, tomato purée and stock, bring to the boil and leave to cook gently. Drain the okra and pat dry, then melt remaining butter in a pan, lightly turn the peppers, courgettes and okra; remove casserole from heat and now add to it these vegetables, half the parsley, the herbs, salt and pepper. A little extra stock may need to be added; bring back to the boil and then place in medium oven for about 45 minutes to one hour, or until meat tender. If fresh peas used, put them in casserole about 15 minutes or as long as required to cook, before completion; if frozen, place in colander, pour on boiling water, drain till dry, then add to cook for about 5 to 10 minutes. Remove when ready, adjust seasoning and stir in parsley.

Etli Türlü
(Meat Stew)

. . . .

SERVES 4

750 grammes lamb, veal or lean
  beef, cut in small cubes
2 large onions or about 10 baby
  onions
2 carrot sliced
2 potatoes peeled and cubed
2 courgettes, sliced
2 tomatoes, chopped
handful of peas - optional
a few okra - optional
olive oil for bottom of pan
pinch of mixed herbs
approx. 1 glass water or stock to
  cover
1/2 teaspoon salt
1/4 teaspoon pepper

   Soften onions in oil; add meat, turn
quickly to brown; add all vegetables
except peas and tomato. Turn to
cover with pan juices and add salt,
pepper and herbs. After a few minutes, pour on water or stock, lower
heat and leave to cook gently for
about 45 minuets; add peas and tomato and if necessary a little more
water and continue to cook until tender. Adjust seasoning and serve with
rice.

Kıymalı Pırasa
(Leeks with Minced Meat)

SERVES 4

This is a good example of one of the many Turkish dishes in which meat and vegetables are cooked together and transform very simple ingredients into a delicious meal.

1 kilo leeks, well washed, cut in thick
   slices
100 grammes mincemeat
1 carrot
2 onions, chopped
4 tablespoons butter
½ glass meat stock

¼ bunch parsley, chopped
¼ bunch dill, chopped
juice of half a lemon
pinch of sugar
salt
black pepper

Place carrots in pan and just cover with water, add a little salt, sugar and 1 spoon of butter; bring to the boil, cover and cook for a few minutes, removing when still firm, but slightly cooked. Melt remaining butter and lightly fry onions; add the meat and turn to brown; then add the leeks and turn lightly until they just start to cook and then add the carrots, stock, salt, pepper and half the dill and parsley. Cover and leave to simmer until the vegetables are tender. Stir in the remaining parsley and dill, briefly raise the heat and when bubbling gently, add lemon juice, freshly ground black pepper and salt if needed.

Kuru Fasulye
(Bean Casserole)

. . . .

SERVES 4

*200 grammes dried haricot beans,
  soaked overnight*
6 glasses water (to boil beans)
2 onions, chopped
2 cloves garlic, crushed
2 tomatoes, skinned and chopped
*1 sweet green pepper, seeded,
  chopped OR 2 small long
  peppers, chopped*

4 glasses meat stock
1 tablespoon tomato purée
1/2 bunch parsley
1 teaspoon paprika
1/2 teaspoon cayenne or chili flakes
pinch of sugar
1 teaspoon salt
ground black pepper

   Drain and rinse beans, then boil in water until tender. Drain, rinse in warm water drain again. Melt butter in a casserole, soften onions and garlic; sprinkle on the paprika and cayenne or chili flakes, stir in well, then add tomatoes and sweet peppers and sugar, stir and cook briefly; add to casserole the beans, tomato purée, warmed stock, parsley, salt and pepper. Cover and cook until beans are soft; if necessary, simmer uncovered to slightly reduce and thicken sauce; adjust seasoning before serving hot. Slices of *sucuk* or any spicy sausage can be added for a more substantial dish.

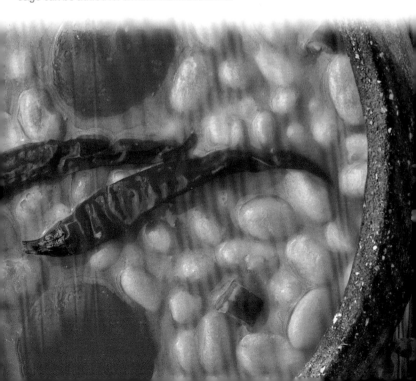

ET VE TAVUK
(MEAT AND CHICKEN)

Lamb is the most widely eaten meat although of course others are used, particularly chicken, often seen roasting on spits, to be bought ready prepared. Many dishes incorporate vegetables, either mixed with meat or stuffed, when they are eaten hot accompanied by yoghurt; the latter is also frequently used as a sauce, alone or with other ingredients.

Adana Kebabı
(Spicy Grilled Meatballs)

• •

SERVES 4

A speciality of Adana in the eastern Mediterranean region; in this part of Turkey and further south and east, which lie closer to the Arab countries, the food is more spicy than elsewhere.

1 kg. minced lamb
3 onions, 2 finely chopped, 1 cut in
  fine rings
3 chili peppers, seeded, finely
  chopped
4 red or green sweet peppers, if long
  ones not available, use round,
  halved and seeded
4 tomatoes, quartered

3 cloves garlic, crushed
1 bunch parsley
1 teaspoon chili powder
2 teaspoons sumak
1 ½ teaspoons salt
1 teaspoon black pepper
pide or other flat bread- 2 to 4
  depending on size
2 tablespoons melted butter

Mix together meat, chopped onions, chili peppers, garlic, most of parsley, chili powder, half the *sumak*, salt and pepper. Knead well until a smooth paste consistency; place in fridge for about 15 minutes. Divide into 8 balls and then work around the skewers, which should have flat blades, moulding the meat so that it is a long sausage shape surrounding the blade. Grill over a charcoal fire or under grill, until well done; also grill the tomato and the sweet peppers. Warm bread, break in pieces, lay on serving dish and pour over the melted butter. Lay the kebabs on bread and arrange tomatoes and peppers on top, then onion rings and scatter with remaining parsley and sumak.

Urfa Kebabı / Fıstıklı Şiş Köfte
(Urfa Meatballs on Skewers / Pistachio Meatballs on Skewers)

• •

As in the case of Adana *kebabı*, that from the town of Urfa in the south-east, is something of a misnomer, as it too does not have pieces of meat, but a sausage shaped meatball. To make it even more confusing, the same shaped meatball which includes pistachio, is called *fıstıklı şiş köfte*.

Urfa Kebabı

basic meatball recipe (p. 86)
replace thyme with paprika add 1
  teaspoon sumak

and an extra clove garlic
pide
a little meat broth
long sweet peppers

Using flat skewers, work the meat round the skewers as for Adana *kebabı*. Break the pide in pieces and lightly grill or toast; then place on dish, pour warmed broth over the pide and when soaked in, lay *kebabs* on top and garnish with grilled peppers.

Fıstıklı Kebab

basic meatball recipe (p. 86)	finely chopped pistachio nuts
leave out thyme add 2 tablespoons	2 extra teaspoons pistachio nuts

Proceed as above and sprinkle nuts on meat half way through grilling.

Tavuk Kanat Şiş
(Grilled Chicken Wings on Skewers)

∙∙

SERVES 4

Chicken wings can either be served as part of a mixed grill or as a little appetizer at an informal meal.

12 chicken wings
marinade for grilled chops (p. 74)
*   with following changes: several*
*   sprigs of fresh lemon thyme*

instead of rosemary
grated rind of a lemon
juice of half a lemon

Prepare the marinade and meat as for chops; thread 6 wings onto each of the skewers; sprinkle with salt, freshly ground black pepper, thyme and lemon thyme before grilling. If using a charcoal grill, place some lemon thyme under the wings.

Kaburga
(Grilled Ribs)

. . . .

SERVES 4

Ribs can be served either as an individual course, preceding the main dish or as part of a mixed grill. They are also a useful addition to a barbecue.

1 kg. ribs
marinade for grilled chops (p. 74)
  with following changes:
1 extra clove garlic, crushed
1 ¹/₂ teaspoons cayenne instead of

the thyme
1 ¹/₂ teaspoons sumak instead of the
  rosemary
¹/₂ tablespoon tomato paste
increase oil by 1 tablespoon

Reserving half a teaspoon of each of the cayenne and sumak, prepare marinade and meat in same way as for chops. Sprinkle with a salt, freshly ground black pepper and the half teaspoons of cayenne and *sumak* before grilling.

Şiş Kebabı / Tavuk / Dana Eti Şiş
(Grilled Lamb on Skewers / Chicken / Veal)

SERVES 4 TO 6

Kebap originally meant meat that was turned over fire, but has come to mean pieces of meat cooked in a variety of ways. As for instance here, on a skewer or *şiş*, when it is *şiş kebabı*. As lamb is the most frequently eaten meat, *şiş kebabı* is effectively lamb *şiş*; when otherwise, the name of the meat is given, *as* in *tavuk şiş*, chicken, *dana eti, şiş,* veal etc. For all versions, pieces of meat are threaded on skewers, alone or with vegetables such as tomatoes, peppers, onions or anything that is good grilled, whichever form it takes, it is best served with rice and salad.

1 kg. lamb, boned and cubed OR
*   meat of choice (chicken, veal etc)*
2 onions
2 cloves garlic
6 tablespoons olive oil

6 tablespoons yoghurt
1 teaspoon salt
1/2 teaspoon black pepper
1 teaspoon thyme

Place the cubed meat in a marinade made of all the above ingredients. Cover and leave in a cold larder or fridge overnight. Thread meat on skewers and grill on both sides over a charcoal fire or under an electric grill.

Pirzola
(Grilled Chops)

SERVES 4

These may either be cooked under a grill or over charcoal, in which case they should be placed on skewers. Lamb is the usual meat, but large chicken joints or beef cutlets are just as good. Muslims do not eat pork, but it could also be used.

8 to 12 chops
2 onions, very finely chopped
1 clove garlic, crushed
4 tablespoons olive oil

2 teaspoons thyme
2 teaspoons bruised dried rosemary
1 teaspoon salt
1/2 teaspoon black pepper

Mix together onion, garlic, 1 teaspoon thyme, 1 teaspoon rosemary, salt, pepper and olive oil; brush on the chops and leave them to stand in any residue for about an hour. Sprinkle chops with salt, black pepper, the second spoons of thyme and rosemary and then grill. Serve with salad and sautéd potatoes.

Çoban Kavurması
(Shepherds' Braised Lamb)

SERVES 5 TO 6

In the past, this dish was made with lamb that had been salted and preserved together with its tail fat. It is called after shepherds because it was they who first used this method of preserving meat which they cooked on a *sac*, a convex griddle. This is also a traditional way of preparing meat from the sacrificial sheep at *Kurban Bayramı*, the Muslim Feast of Sacrifice, commemorating Abraham's sacrifice. Dripping from roast lamb can be used, though it will not have quite the same flavour.

1 kg. lamb, boned, cut in small cubes
75 grammes tail fat (dripping or butter)
chopped vegetables such as mushrooms, onions, peppers, tomatoes etc.
thyme
salt
black pepper

Melt the fat, add the meat, brown, add the vegetables and thyme, turn to lightly brown; cover and cook over low heat, stirring occasionally, until tender. When ready, sprinkle with salt and pepper and a little more thyme.

NOTE: at the *bayram*, the kidney and diced liver are added

Ilgaz Kebabı
(*Ilgaz* Grilled Meat)

· ·

SERVES 4

The way in which this dish is arranged, symbolises *Ilgaz Dağı*, a mountain near the town of Kastamonu in north-central Anatolia, inland from the Black Sea. The mound of rice piled in the centre represents the mountain and the melted cheese is the snow; as the slopes of the mountain are heavily forested, the parsley symbolises the trees; the meat is the earth and the green peppers and tomato are the wild flowers most charmingly, the lovely beauty and freshness of the mountain.

4 to 6 cups cooked rice
Freshly grilled meat of choice
150 to 200 grammes grated cheese
  (kaşar, cheddar etc.)
a few sprigs of parsley
1 tomato sliced or quartered
1 or 2 green peppers sliced or
  halved depending on shape

Choose a heatproof dish suitable for the arrangement and pile the rice in a mound in the centre. Lay the cooked meat around it and then put grated cheese on top, Place under grill and when the cheese just starts to melt, remove and arrange the tomato and peppers and return to grill. When the cheese is fully melted, remove and arrange the parsley.

Yoğurtlu Kebap
(Kebab with Yoghurt)

• •

SERVES 6

This dish, consists of meat placed on *pide* which has been co-vered with a tomato sauce and yoghurt. There are no hard and fast rules as to how the meat should be cooked or indeed which meat. Grilled meat is generally used, but it does not matter whether it is lamb or chicken, *şiş*, meatballs, cubes or slices from a larger piece, all are equally delicious when combined with the sauce and yoghurt.

1 kg. lamb or meat of choice
6 pide
500 gr. yoghurt
4 large tomatoes, skinned and
*   chopped*
1 onion, chopped
2 chili peppers
1 aubergine sliced OR tomato and
*   pepper, sliced*
2 cloves garlic, crushed
3 tablespoons butter
pinch of sugar
2 to 3 tablespoons water
1 teaspoon sumak
1 teaspoon thyme
salt
pepper

While the meat is cooking, prepare the tomato sauce: using 1 spoon of butter, soften the onion, then add tomatoes, chili peppers, garlic, salt, pepper, sugar and after a little while, add all or some of the water depending on con-sistency. Fry the aubergine strips or lightly turn the tomato and pepper slices in the rest of the butter.Cut the pide into quarters and place on warmed dish. Spoon the tomato sauce onto the pide; beat the yoghurt and pour this over the tomato and pide: arrange the meat on top and then garnish with the aubergine or tomato and pepper slices and sprinkle with thyme and sumak.

Beğendili Kebab
(Lamb with Aubergine Purée)

SERVES 6

Also known as *Hünkar Beğendi*, meaning 'the monarch approved', this is an excellent combination of lamb and aubergine.

1 kilo leg of lamb, cubed
2 onions, finely chopped
3 tomatoes, skinned and chopped
1 green pepper, seeded and
  chopped
½ kilo aubergine
2 cloves garlic, crushed
2 glasses meat stock

2 glasses warm milk
200 grammes butter
3 tablespoons flour
4 tablespoons grated kaşar cheese
  (or cheddar, gruyère)
1 ½ teaspoons salt
½ teaspoon black pepper
nutmeg

Melt 75 grammes butter in a large pan, soften onions; add meat and turn over medium heat. Then add garlic and green pepper. When beginning to soften, add tomatoes, stock, salt and pepper, bring to the boil; cover and leave to simmer over low heat for about an hour or until meat tender (in pressure cooker, about half an hour). Meanwhile make aubergine purée: prick aubergines, cook over charcoal or gas flame until skins are charred and flesh tender. Scrape away skin and chop pulp. Melt remaining butter in another pan and stir in flour to make a roux. Add aubergines to roux and mash well; then place on heat and cook gently; add warm milk, stirring all the time; when bubbling, add cheese and sesoning; keep stirring for a little and after a couple of minutes, remove and sprinkle in nutmeg. Pour purée on serving dish, make a hollow and arrange meat in centre.

KÖFTELER
(MEATBALLS)

Kuru Köfte
(Fried Meatballs)

● ●

SERVES 4 TO 6

A traditional dish at Turkish picnics, these meatballs keep well in the fridge but they are equally good served hot, with salad and fried potatoes.

500 grammes minced meat
3 slices stale white bread, crusts
   removed
1 onion, very finely chopped
1 clove garlic, finely crushed
1 egg, beaten

¹/₃ bunch parsley, finely chopped
¹/₂ teaspoon cumin
1 teaspoon salt
¹/₂ teaspoon black pepper
50 grammes flour
1 cup sunflower oil

Soak the bread in a little water, then squeeze away excess moisture and crumble over the meat. Mix together meat with bread, onion, garlic, egg, parsley, cumin, salt and pepper and knead very well. Wet palms with water and shape into thick fingers. Sprinkle flour onto a board or tray and roll the fingers until covered lightly. Heat oil in pan and fry until the *köfte* are brown.

Patates Köftesi
(Potato Balls)

● ●

SERVES 4

6 medium potatoes, peeled, chopped
200 grammes grated kaşar cheese
   (cheddar, gruyère)
2 eggs and 2 yolks
75 grammes flour or breadcrumbs

grated nutmeg
salt
pepper
oil for frying

Boil and mash the potatoes. Add cheese, 2 egg yolks, nutmeg, salt and pepper, then mix well and shape into balls or sausage shapes. Place on tray sprinkled with half the flour, shake very gently and sprinkle with remaining flour. Dip into beaten eggs, then roll in breadcrumbs and fry in hot oil.

Kadınbudu Köfte
(Lady's Thighs Meatballs)

SERVES 4 TO 6

This form of meatball acquired its name as a compliment to ladies, in the days when they were well regarded if gently rounded. For ladies who are happy to be so, or for men who happily like them so, cook, eat and enjoy.

500 grammes minced meat
50 grammes rice
1 1/2 cups water
1 onion, very finely chopped
2 tablespoons butter
2 eggs

1/2 bunch parsley, finely chopped
1/2 teaspoon allspice
salt
pepper
50 grammes flour
1 cup sunflower oil

Cook rice in the water until tender, then drain. Soften the onions in butter, add half the meat and stir until cooked; then remove from heat, add the remaining meat, rice, 1 beaten egg, parsley, allspice, salt and pepper, mix well and knead thoroughly. Shape into small oval pieces and flatten. Dip into flour and then into the second beaten egg; fry in hot oil on both sides until golden brown. Serve hot with salad.

Domates Soslu Köfte
(Meatballs in Tomato Sauce)

SERVES 4 TO 6

¹/₂ bunch dill
basic meatball recipe (p. 86)
4 large tomatoes, skinned and
    chopped
2 cloves garlic, crushed
¹/₂ bunch parsley

2 tablespoons tomato paste
1 glass water
2 tablespoons butter or olive oil
pinch of sugar
salt
pepper

Add dill to the meatball recipe and make small meatballs; either grill or lightly fry in a little butter or olive oil, but do not cook completely. Soften onions in butter or oil; add garlic and after a couple of minutes, the tomatoes; cook uncovered for a few minutes and then add sugar, salt, pepper, tomato paste and most of water. Then place in the meatballs and cook for about 15 to 20 minutes. Stir in the parsley, adjust seasoning and serve with rice or noodles and salad.

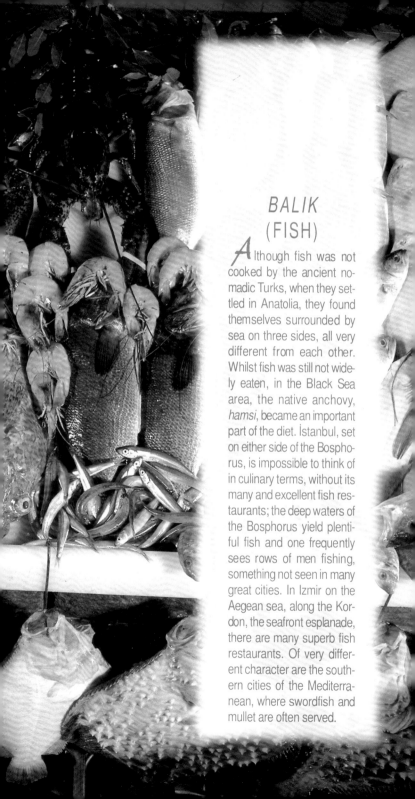

BALIK
(FISH)

*A*lthough fish was not cooked by the ancient nomadic Turks, when they settled in Anatolia, they found themselves surrounded by sea on three sides, all very different from each other. Whilst fish was still not widely eaten, in the Black Sea area, the native anchovy, *hamsi*, became an important part of the diet. İstanbul, set on either side of the Bosphorus, is impossible to think of in culinary terms, without its many and excellent fish restaurants; the deep waters of the Bosphorus yield plentiful fish and one frequently sees rows of men fishing, something not seen in many great cities. In Izmir on the Aegean sea, along the Kordon, the seafront esplanade, there are many superb fish restaurants. Of very different character are the southern cities of the Mediterranean, where swordfish and mullet are often served.

Lüfer Izgara
(Grilled Bluefish)

SERVES 4

Lüfer is given different names depending on its size or age; çinekop is the small, young fish, *kofana* is the large and the medium is *sarı kanat* and *koruk lüferi*. This fish is especially popular in Istanbul, being found in the Bosphorus, to which it is indigenous.

4 lüfer	juice of a lemon
1 onion, finely chopped	1 teaspoon mustard
1 tomato, skinned and chopped	4 lemon wedges
1/4 bunch chopped parsley	salt
fresh thyme or bay leaves	pepper
125 ml. olive oil	

The fish should be gutted, with the scales removed and well washed. Brush with olive oil, sprinkle with salt; insert herbs or bay leaf in slit on edge of abdomen. Grill or bake; mix tomato, onion and parsley, season and place next to fish; place wedges of lemon on each plate and serve with dressing made from olive oil, lemon, mustard, salt and pepper. Though rosemary is not much used in Turkish cooking, it goes very well with fish — either lay long sprigs under fish when grilling or insert in slit, or sprinkle with rubbed dried herb.

Karides
(Shrimps)

These delicate flavoured shell fish, somewhat larger than in northern Europe, are excellent, shelled and quickly tossed in a little hot butter with lemon juice squeezed into the pan while lightly turning; cook very briefly just so that the lemon, which will quickly reduce in the heat, slightly flavours the shrimps. Serve immediately with lemon pieces.

Kalamar Dolma
(Stuffed Squid)

STUFFING FOR 4 HEADS

This delicious dish can be made if you can get fresh large squid or baby octopus. Have them prepared, the tentacles cut off, so that the 'head/foot' is cleaned and ready to stuff.

200 grammes finely chopped squid,	2 tablespoons fish stock
1 onion, chopped	nut of butter
2 tomatoes, skinned and chopped	olive oil
4 cloves garlic, chopped	salt
2 teaspoons tomato purée	pepper
1/4 bunch parsley, chopped	

Soften onions and two thirds of chopped garlic; add squid pieces, turn lightly; add most of the parsley, purée and stock; simmer and reduce. Then stuff the squids and skewer with a toothpick. Heat olive oil in pan; if the reduction has been properly done, use the same pan, as this adds flavour; add remaining garlic and lightly sauté the stuffed squids until cooked. Do not overcook or this toughens them.

Kalkan Tava
(Fried Turbot)

Along the Bosphorus and the sea of Marmara there are many excellent fish restaurants, serving fish caught the same day. Turbot is usually served fried, either filleted or left whole, or cut in slices on the bone. It is simply sprinkled with salt, then dipped in flour and fried in sunflower oil. Serve with lemon wedges and dressed salad. Sole (*dil balığı*) and the good flavoured, but bony small red mullet (*barbunya*) are also good prepared this way.

Balık Buğulama
(Poached Fish)

....

SERVES 6

Sea bass (*levrek*),
bluefish (*lüfer*), grey mullet
(*kefal*) and gurnard (*kırlangıç*),
are all very good when poached. Depending on size and type
of fish, it can be filleted or left whole.

sufficient fish of choice
1 kilo tomatoes, skinned,
chopped
2 onions chopped
2 cloves garlic, chopped
200 grammes mushrooms,
button or sliced if larger
125 ml. fish stock
50 grammes butter
3/4 bunch dill, chopped
juice of 1 lemon
bayleaves
salt
pepper
freshly boiled potatoes

Prepare fish (gut, wash, drain); sprinkle
with salt and lemon juice. In a large deep
frying pan or pan for poaching, gently soften
onions and garlic in butter, add the mushrooms,
cook a bit longer, then add tomatoes and soften; push
some to one side, but leave enough on pan base to create
a bed to lay the fish on; arrange vegetables around and on top
of fish and add the stock, most of the dill, bayleaves, salt and pepper. Cover and poach for about 10 to 15 minutes, depending on fish size.
About half way through cooking, uncover and place the boiled potatoes in the
sauce, so that they absorb the flavours; before serving, sprinkle with remaining dill.

Kılıç Şiş
(Swordfish on Skewers)

SERVES 4 TO 6

Swordfish is very good in Turkey and being very firm fleshed, is excellent for grilling in steaks or on skewers.

750 grammes boned swordfish
1 large tomato
1 green pepper
1 onion, finely chopped
2 cloves garlic, crushed
2 lemons cut in thin slices
¹/₂ tablespoon lemon juice

175 ml. olive oil
¹/₂ tablespoon tomato purée
¹/₂ teaspoon dried thyme or crushed
  rosemary
bayleaves
salt
pepper

Have the swordfish boned and skinned; cut into large cubes, about 3 cm. Make a marinade of olive oil, lemon juice, tomato purée, onion, garlic, herbs, bayleaves soaked in water for an hour beforehand, salt and pepper. Leave fish in marinade for at least half an hour, though a couple of hours is better. Remove and thread fish onto skewers, alternating with slices of tomato, pepper, lemon and bayleaf. Grill over charcoal or under hot electric grill, turning frequently and basting with marinade; this takes about 15 to 20 minutes. Serve with slices of lemon and salad.

PİLAVLAR
(RICE DISHES)

R ice is extensively used to make *pilav*, with a variety of ingredients added, to make a more or less substantial dish, served either as an accompaniment or as an individual course. Long grained rice is the most suitable for *pilav*, which is usually cooked a little in oil or butter before water or stock is added.

Meyhane Pilavı
(Cracked Wheat (*Bulgur*) & Meat Pilaf)

SERVES 4

200 grammes bulgur
150 grammes meat in very small cubes
1 onion, finely chopped
2 green peppers (capsicum/ pepperone) seeded & chopped
2 sticks celery, finely chopped

2 tomatoes, skinned and chopped
1 ¹/₂ glasses meat or chicken stock
1 glass tomato juice
¹/₂ bunch parsley, finely chopped
salt
pepper
butter

Wash and drain the *bulgur* and place aside. Melt butter and when hot, quickly turn meat in it and then add onion, green peppers and celery and sauté a little, before adding the tomato. Cook briefly and then pour in the stock and tomato juice and bring to the boil. Add the *bulgur* and quickly stir it. Reduce heat and cook gently until all moisture is absorbed. Remove from heat, add most of the parsley. Cover the saucepan and leave to stand for about an hour. Serve hot, garnished with parsley.

Sebzeli Pilav
(Rice with Vegetables)

SERVES 4

200 grammes long grained rice
200 grammes peas
1 large onion, chopped
2 carrots, chopped
2 sticks celery, chopped
2 tablespoons butter

2 glasses (500 ml) chicken stock or dissolved cube
1 ¹/₂ teaspoons salt - less if cube used
black pepper

Melt butter and lightly sauté onion, carrots and celery for a few minutes. Now add the rice and stir for a couple more minutes, making sure that all the grains are coated. Then pour in the stock and add salt and pepper. Cover and bring to the boil. After a few moments, remove and if the peas are big and not young they may be added now. Then turn heat very low, cover and leave to cook until all the water has been absorbed. If frozen peas are used, or very young ones, these should be cooked separately and carefully stirred into the rice before serving.

Nohutlu Pilav
(Rice with Chickpeas)

• •

SERVES 4

200 grammes long grained rice
75 grammes chickpeas
1 onion
2 ½ glasses (625 ml) chicken stock
  or water

2 tablespoons butter
½ teaspoon allspice
½ teaspoon cinnamon
1 ½ teaspoons salt
black pepper

  Soak chickpeas overnight; rinse, drain and then cook in salted water for about 40 minutes, or until partially cooked. Melt butter, soften onion, then add the rice and turn until all the grains are coated. Add the drained chickpeas, stock or water, spices and salt. Bring to the boil and then cook over low heat until all the moisture is absorbed. Garnish with freshly ground black pepper and a sprinkling of cinnamon.

Sarı Pilav
(Rice with Saffron)

. . . .

SERVES 4

200 grammes long grained rice
1 onion
2 glasses chicken stock or water
a few strands of saffron
OR 1 teaspoon turmeric
2 tablespoons butter
4 tablespoons raisins

2 tablespoons pine nuts - optional
½ teaspoon allspice
3 or 4 cloves
1 teaspoon coriander seeds, lightly
  crushed
1 ½ teaspoons salt
black pepper

   Melt butter and cook onion lightly; add the rice and cook for a few minutes, turning to coat all the grains. Place the saffron in a small bowl or saucer with a little water and set aside. Now pour stock or water onto the rice and add all the spices, salt, pepper, raisins and pine nuts and either the turmeric or saffron (tip in the contents of the bowl or saucer, merely subtracting the same quantity from the stock). Cover, bring to the boil and after a minute or so, turn very low and cook until moisture is absorbed.

HAMUR İŞLERİ (PASTRY)

*S*avoury pastry dishes form a large category of Turkish food and pasta was borrowed from the Chinese before the Turks came to Anatolia. It takes various forms, such as mantı, little stuffed dumplings and the similar dish, *tatar böreği* and *erişte*, noodles, which are combined with a wide range of ingredients. But of all such dishes, *börek* reigns supreme today, as in Ottoman times, when there were laws regulating the quality of *börek* sold to the public. Made from layers of finely rolled sheets of dough, *yufka*, which can be bought, between which is a filling of cheese or meat, *börek* comes in many shapes and sizes. In most western countries phyllo pastry, which is the same, can be bought.

Cevizli Erişte
(Noodles with Cheese and Walnuts)

An unusual way of serving pasta, this simple dish is not for those watching their figures, but it is delicious.

500 grammes noodles or any pasta shape
3 to 4 tablespoons butter
2 tablespoons olive oil
250 grammes grated mature kaşar

(cheddar, gruyère)
150 grammes walnuts, chopped
½ teaspoon nutmeg
salt
freshly ground black pepper

Boil noodles in plenty of boiling salted water; when *al dente* drain, pour on hot water, drain again and place on serving dish with the olive oil in it and blend lightly. Keep back a little cheese and then stir in cheese, nuts, melted butter and nutmeg; sprinkle with plenty of freshly ground black pepper.

Mantı
(Meat Dumplings with Yoghurt)

●●

SERVES 4

Sometimes called Turkish ravioli, these little dumplings are indeed similar to the Italian dish. This is hardly surprising, as both versions of stuffed pasta parcels were borrowed from China, but the Turks of central Asia were cooking pasta long before it reached Italy. Lazy cooks could use good quality meat filled ravioli and make the Turkish sauce, though of course it isn't quite the same.

DOUGH:

250 grammes flour
1 teaspoon salt
1 egg
2 tablespoons oil
3 tablespoons water

SAUCE:

500 grammes yoghurt
3 cloves garlic, crushed

FILLING:

225 grammes minced lamb
1 onion, grated
salt
pepper
2 ½ litres water for boiling
½ teaspoon salt

DRESSING SAUCE:

5 tablespoons butter, melted
2 tomatoes, skinned, finely chopped
1 clove garlic, crushed
1 tesaspoon paprika
1 teaspoon dried mint
salt

First prepare filling: mix all ingredients in a bowl. To make dumplings: Place flour and salt in bowl and mix together. Make a well in centre and pour in oil, egg and water; mix the liquids and gradually incorporate flour, working with fingertips; then knead to a stiff paste. Cover with a napkin and set aside for half an hour. Divide in two; using a floured board, knead again and shape each into a round ball. Set aside one round and cover; roll out the other into long strips, about 3 to 4 cm. wide and then cut into squares. Place meat filling in the centre of each square, gather the opposite corners together, pinching firmly, to make little bundles. Repeat procedure with second ball of dough.

Bring water to the boil and add salt. Place in the bundles carefully and stir occasionally to prevent them sticking; they take about 15 minutes to cook and will rise to surface when ready.

Remove 3 to 4 tablespoons of liquid to a bowl; drain the dumplings and place on heated dish. Pour the reserved liquid over them and then the yoghurt, into which garlic has been beaten.

Finally pour over this, a sauce made of melted butter in which tomatoes and garlic have been softened and to which paprika, dried mint and a little salt and pepper have been added.

Saray Katmeri
(Spinach and Crèpes Gratin)

SERVES 4 TO 6

Best described as a cross between a roulade and lasagna, this is an excellent first course or light main course.

10 to 12 large crèpes (use a thin
   pancake mixture)
1 kg. spinach
150 grammes butter
250 grammes grated kaşar cheese
   (gruyère)
200 grammes lebne (fromage frais/

   sour cream)
2 eggs, beaten
1/2 to 1 teaspoon nutmeg
1 to 2 teaspoons paprika
salt
pepper

Boil the spinach, plunge in cold water to keep the colour, then drain well, squeeze excess liquid, chop and mash in half the butter; stir in lebne, nutmeg, eggs, a little salt (depending on how salty the cheese) and pepper. Butter a deep cake pan, a loose ring one is best, or a baking sheet and deep ring; then sprinkle with some grated cheese and paprika. Make large crèpes/very thin pancakes. Place in tin, with a layer of filling sprinkled with a little cheese, until reaching near the top and finish with a thick layer of cheese and paprika. The quantities may need adjusting slightly. Bake in medium oven for about 15 minutes, until cheese is melted and has formed a light crust. Release spring or lift ring and return to oven for a few minutes to allow the side to brown a little, but this is not vital.

Sigara Böreği
(Rolls)

SERVES 4

2 sheets yufka (phyllo)
250 ml. oil for frying
OR 50 grammes melted butter if
  baking
FILLING:
200 grammes crumbled white

cheese
1 tablespoon grated kaşar cheese
  (parmesan)
1 egg yolk
1/4 bunch parsley, chopped
1/4 bunch dill, chopped

Divide the pastry sheets into two equal semi-circles and then each into four triangles. Place filling at the base of each and then roll it up like a cigarette, wet the pointed end and stick it down. Fry in hot oil till golden OR brush tops with melted butter and bake on greased baking sheet in moderate oven until golden and crips, about 15 minutes.

NOTE: sage is also good with cheese; other fillings include savoury mince, spinach and cheese, etc.

Kabak Böreği
(Courgette and Cheese Börek)

SERVES 4 TO 6

6 sheets yufka (phyllo pastry)
2 courgettes, very finely chopped/ grated
1 small onion, very finely chopped
1 clove garlic, crushed -optional
250 grammes crumbled white cheese
300 grammes yoghurt

200 ml. milk
250 grammes butter
6 eggs
1/2 bunch parsley, chopped
1/2 bunch dill
salt
pepper

Prepare filling: sprinkle salt on courgettes and drain for an hour or so; squeeze excess liquid, combine with onion, garlic, cheese, 3 beaten eggs, parsley, dill, salt and pepper; set aside. Beat remaining 3 eggs in a bowl and combine with yoghurt, milk and melted butter. Lay one yufka in a large circular baking sheet with raised edges, so that the edges of the yufka overhang; spread on a little of the yoghurt/egg/butter mixture; divide second yufka into large pieces, lay over first and spread yoghurt mix; then lay the whole third yufka, with edges hanging over and spread all courgette/cheese filling, and on top, a little yoghurt mix; divide fourth and fifth yufka into large pieces, lay over filling and spread with yoghurt mix; lay sixth yufka on top and then plenty of yoghurt mixture. Fold the edges in and brush with remaining mix, to seal. Cover with damp cloth and leave for about 25 minutes; bake in moderate oven till puffed up and golden, about 40 minutes.

Lahmacun
(Savoury Flat Bread)

SERVES 6

Sold in countless little shops and kiosks, this is a delicious little meal with salad or a snack; usually it is rolled up, wrapped in a little slip of paper and eaten standing at a kiosk.

3 glasses flour
3 glasses water
250 grammes minced lamb
1 onion, finely chopped
1/2 bunch parsley, chopped

1/2 teaspoon salt
2 puddingspoons water for filling
glass of water for yeast
1 puddingspoon yeast
1 puddingspoon sugar

Mix the yeast and sugar in a bowl with a glass of tepid water and leave overnight, making sure it is not in a cold place. Make a dough from the flour, water and yeast, which must be kneaded very well and then divided into equal portions; leave for a while and then roll until each is as thin as an ear lobe - there is no other way of describing this. Mix the meat, onion, parsley salt and water and spread on each piece of dough; ideally, place in open fire oven, but as this is unlikely to be to hand, bake at a moderate heat for about 10 minutes. A little mixed herbs or thyme is good added to the meat.

LOKUM
(TURKISH DELIGHT)

TATLILAR
(DESSERTS)

*T*urkish puddings and confections are justly famous and it is often the case that people who have tried the preparations that pass for *baklava* or *kadayıf* in the west and have not liked them, change their minds when they eat them in Turkey. The eating of sweet dishes is deeply entrenched in Turkish culture and traditionally they were not only eaten as a course of the meal. Births, circumcisions, engagements, weddings, religious festivals and many other events, even deaths and funerals all have their own special sweets or puddings.

Although the most famous is *baklava*, there are many other pastries made of the fine *yufka* pastry leaves, such as the charmingly named *bülbül yuvası*, 'nightingale's nest'. And who could resist 'beauty's lips', *dilber dudağı*, or 'lady's navel', *hanım göbeği*? As with the tiny sausage shaped *tulumba*, they are made of a dough which is fried and then turned in syrup. There are also many milk puddings and fruit based dishes, using either fresh or dried fruits and

nuts are widely used as part of many puddings.

Helva, best known in the west in the pressed sesame form, which is commercially produced, comes in many varieties; it is not easy to make, though it seems very simple, being made from only various forms of flour, butter, sugar and flavouring. *Lokum* or 'Turkish Delight' is another favourite sweetmeat often flavoured with rosewater or mint, it is thickened with mastic nowadays made commercially.

Still found in some cities and towns, although less than formerly, are the puddings shops or *muhallebici,* meaning milkpudding sellers, which is what they were originally. In the past, and even now, in small towns, milk puddings and pastries were sold in different shops, but today they sell milk puddings, pastries and beverages. In more traditional places, in winter only *salep,* a delicious milk drink thickened with powdered orchid root, is on offer, replaced in summer by ice-cream, *dondurma*; otherwise its water or soft drinks. *Salep* is used to thicken this sticky and scrumptious ice-cream, for which the city of Kahramanmaraş is famous.

Aşure
(Noah's Pudding)

. . . .

SERVES 8

Combining grains, nuts and fruits,
this is the pudding that Noah is said
to have invented, when using what-
ever food was left in the Ark, he and
his family celebrated the receding of
the flood waters. It is also made and
eaten to commemorate the death of
Mohammed's grandson.

120 grammes whole wheat kernels
100 grammes dried white beans
70 grammes chickpeas
50 grammes rice
250 grammes sugar
10 dried figs
10 dried apricots
50 grammes raisins
50 grammes sultanas
50 grammes almonds, blanched
50 grammes walnuts
50 grammes pistachio nuts
2 tablespoons pine nuts
grated peel of 1 orange
2 tablespoons rosewater
seeds from 1 pomegranate

Soak wheat and pulses overnight
in water, in separate bowls; drain,
rinse and cook each seperately until
tender, then drain and save the cooking liquids. Put wheat and pulses and
rice in this liquid, add water if necessary and cook for about an hour.
Add sugar and orange peel and simmer till sugar dissolved. Chop figs
and apricots that have been soaked
and add them, raisins and sultanas
to the mixture. Simmer for 10 minutes and add rosewater. Chill and stir
in nuts and pomegranate seeds.

Ayva Tatlısı
(Quince Dessert)

• •

SERVES 6

Apart from making excellent jam and jelly, quinces make an interesting sweet. Slabs of sugar flavoured with spices and dyed red called *lohusa şekeri* are sold in Turkish markets; if you can get it, this adds a good flavour and colour to the dish, which is still good without it.

3 quinces
1 apple
500 grammes sugar
juice of a small lemon
500 ml. water

2 to 3 cloves
1 teaspoon cinnamon
50 grammes lohusa şekeri —
  optional
150 grammes kaymak or cream

Peel quinces, cut in half, core and then put in shallow saucepan. Peel and grate the apple over quinces and sprinkle the sugar and cinnamon; then add water, lemon juice, cloves and *lohusa şekeri* if available. Cover and cook over low heat until fruit is tender. Serve cold with *kaymak* or cream.

Kaymaklı Kayısı Tatlısı
(Dried Apricots Stuffed with Cream)

••

SERVES 6

Kaymak traditionally made from buffalo milk, is incredibly thick, calorific and scrumptious. It is reduced from the milk by boiling until it is firm enough to slice. Stuffed into soaked dried apricots it makes an easy and luxurious pudding. This version uses far less sugar, as the tartness of the apricots is lost when they are cooked in a very sweet syrup.

500 grammes dried apricots, soaked overnight
100 grammes sugar
375 ml. water
¹/₂ to 1 teaspoon lemon juice

225 grammes kaymak (or very thick cream)
100 grammes pistachio nuts, finely chopped

Drain the dried apricots; heat water and sugar together and cook for about 7-10 minutes; add apricots and cook till tender, then add lemon juice and cook another couple of minutes. Remove apricots and leave to cool. Split half open, stuff with *kaymak* and arrange on dish; pour syrup over and sprinkle on pistachio nuts.

119

Kabak Tatlısı
(Pumpkin Desert)

• •

SERVES 4

This somewhat resembles a preserve, though it is a pudding and is very good served with *kaymak*.

1 kilo pumpkin flesh (after peeling)
500 grammes sugar
1 ¹/₂ teaspoons cinnamon - optional
pistachio nuts or walnuts to garnish
kaymak or cream

Cut pumpkin into slices, wash and cut into squares of about 2 or 3 cms. Place in large pan, sprinkle sugar between layers. Cook until pumpkin very tender and a syrup has formed, about an hour or more. Put pumpkin and syrup on serving dish and leave to cool, by which time most of the syrup will have been absorbed by the pumpkin. Serve with a little of remaining syrup and *kaymak*.

Keşkül
(Almond Milk Pudding)

• •

SERVES 4

A very simple but good pudding, which can be made even more so by the addition of *kaymak*.

150 grammes almonds, blanched   *¹/₄ glass water*
3 tablespoons ground rice   *2 tablespoons grated coconut*
125 grammes sugar   *1 tablespoon pistachio nuts*
1 litre milk   *kaymak or thick cream*

Grind the almonds coarsely and then pour ¹/₂ glass warmed milk over them to infuse; it is better to use a blender and having ground the almonds, add milk and blend for a few minutes. Either way, transfer the almonds and milk to saucepan and heat. Stir ground rice in water and add to the almonds and milk, stirring constantly and as it begins to thicken add sugar and then coconut. Continue stirring until thick and creamy. Transfer to serving dishes and leave to cool. Garnish with pistachio and ground almond and before serving, some *kaymak*.

BADEM EZMESİ
(ALMOND PASTE)

Vişne Kompostosu / Vişne Ekmek Tatlısı
(Sour Cherry Compote / Sour Cherry Bread Pudding)

SERVES 6

This rather tart fruit, effectively a wild cherry, but now cultivated, from which an excellent drink is made, makes very good compote, which in turn can be used for a bread pudding a reminiscent of summer pudding.

Compote:

500 grammes sour cherries

500 grammes sugar
2 glasses water

Wash cherries, stone, place in pan with water and sugar and bring to boil. If using as compote, leave to cool.

Bread pudding:

1/2 loaf white bread

cherry compote,
hot kaymak or cream

Remove crusts from bread and slice thickly. Lay slices on a baking sheet in preheated oven, 150 degrees C. until lightly browned; lay in serving dish, pour on the compote and leave to cool. Serve with *kaymak*.

Meyva Hoşafı
(Stewed Fruit)

· ·

SERVES 4

There is an abundance of fresh and dried fruit in Turkey and any or several are stewed and known as *hoşaf*. This is a Persian word meaning 'pleasant water' and indeed the juice rather than the fruit is seen as the delicacy, though both are consumed. In the past, aromatic substances, such as musk were added. Interestingly, it is often served after pilaf dishes, also acquired from Persia. Sultanas, cherries, apricots and plums are the most popular forms, although here, dried fruits are used. As a gesture to ancient traditions, a little rose water can be added.

500 grammes dried apricots
500 grammes dried figs
500 grammes any other dried fruit
200 grammes sultanas
100 to 250 grammes sugar,
depending on taste
100 grammes pistachio or pine nuts
water to cover soaked fruits
a little rose water

Soak the fruits overnight. Drain and
then put all in a pan, except the sultanas
and nuts. Cover with water and add the sugar;
cook gently and about half way, add the sultanas. When
soft, remove from heat, add the nuts and rosewater and leave to cool.

Çay
(Turkish Tea)

. . . .

Although the shelves of shops are
filled with various brands of import-
ed tea, the Turks prefer to drink the
local product which grows in the
Black Sea region.

Turkish tea is offered in small glass
cups, and is served from early morn-
ing until late at night. It must be hot
and umber; 'rabbit blood' colour is
the adjective that the Turks employ
to describe its colour.

In order to make it, two teapots are
used. After putting one table spoon
for three or four cups amount of tea
leaves into the smaller tea-pot, it is
placed on top of a larger pot with
water. A small amount from the
boiled water is poured on the tea-
leaves and left to be distilled for about
6 minutes. First the distilled tea is
poured into the cup to its half-length
then hot water is added to the brim.

Türk Kahvesi
(Turkish Coffee)

· ·

Although Turkey does not grow coffee, it is thought that the Turks first introduced this drink to the West and for that reason it was called 'Turkish coffee'.

According to the traditional recipe, it is prepared: *sade* (without sugar), *az şekerli* (with a little sugar), *orta* (medium sweet), or *çok şekerli* (very sweet) and is served in small cups.

To make Turkish coffee you need a *cezve* (a small coffee pot with a long handle) of tin lined copper or other metal.

Use one generous teaspoon of coffee for each cup; stir this, sugar (as above) and water (using the cup for measurement) in the pot. Place over a gentle heat (a gas flame is much the best) and slowly bring to the boil. Watch it carefully and as it begins to boil a thick froth will form on top. Just before it reaches the top, remove pot and carefully pour a little of this froth in each cup. Return pot to the heat and bring it just to the boil again. Pour coffee into cups without disturbing the froth in them - I find it helps if you tremble your hand slightly whilst pouring. Let the sediment settle.

When one makes several cups of coffee it is better to do the froth again at the end.

A glass of water is often served with the coffee; drinking this prepares the palate to digest the coffee.

After drinking, it is pleasant to while away the time predicting the future. The coffee drunk, one gives the cup

The coffee drunk, one gives the cup a little swirl, and then turns it upside down on the saucer, leaving it to be lifted by the person who will read it. It is important that the cup be completely cold if the future is to be read clearly!!!

Rakı

Rakı is distilled from grapes and has an alcohol content of 45 degrees. The anise content, which gives the characteristic flavour, causes it to become milky white when water is added.

One pours water into the rakı and then stirs it with ice.

In Turkey rakı is regarded like a medicine, the cure for many ailments, even snake-bite. The importance of drinking it is never more so than with meze.

Nevertheless it is wise to take heed of the following advice to protect the digestion.

1 glass: you feel like a sultan
2 glasses: you discover unexpected talents
3 glasses: you are able to talk like a Turk
4 glasses: walking straight becomes a problem
5 glasses you don't care where in the world you lie down.

Portakal çayı
Orange tea

Kuşburnu çayı
Dog rose tea

Ihlamur çayı
Linden blossom t

Mandalina çayı
Tangerine tea

Limon çayı
Lemon tea

Böğürtlen çayı
Blackberry tea

İÇECEKLER
(BEVERAGES)

GLOSSARY

Bamya: okra or ladies fingers

Beyaz peynir: white cheese, the same as feta

Börek: various forms of savoury pastry; may be baked, fried or even steamed

Bulgur: cracked wheat

Dolma: stuffed, as in vineleaves and vegetables

Helva: sweetmeat of flour, semolina, sesame, butter, milk, nuts and other flavourings

Kabak: pumpkin, courgette and other squashes

Kadayıf: various forms of sweet pastry

Kaşar peyniri: hard sheep's milk cheese, not unlike cheddar, but milder

Kaymak: similar to clotted cream, very thick rich cream

Köfte: small round or sausage shaped pressed ball of meat ; also meatless of chickpeas etc

Kuru: dry or dried as in beans etc

Lebne or labne: similar to creme fraiche; it is not actually Turkish so much as Lebanese and Syrian; however, useful in some dishes

Levrek: sea bass

Lüfer: similar to bluefish; indigenous to Bosphorus

Nohut: chickpeas

Pastırma: pressed beef preserved in spices

Sirke: vinegar

Sucuk: spicy Turkish sausage

Sumak: a herb with a slightly sour taste

Tatlı: sweet, pudding, confection

Tavuk: chicken, but strictly, a stewing hen

Taze: fresh

Tel kadayıf: strands of dough cooked on a griddle and resembling shredded wheat

Terbiye: a thickening or liasion of egg, lemon and flour

Tereyağı: butter

Tuz: salt

Vişne: sour cherry, like morello cherry.

Yoğurt: Milk crudled by using a bacteria culture; widely used

Yufka: fine sheets of pastry

Zeytinyağlı: vegetables cooked with olive oil; served cold

MEASUREMENTS

A glass is equivalent to a standard cup measure, namely 250 ml. liquid

Tablespoon 15 to 20 gr. butter, sugar, rice; 7 to 8 gr. flour

Puddingspoon (dessert spoon) roughly two thirds above

Teaspoon

INDEX

Tavuk Kanat Şiş (Grilled Chicken Wings on Skewers) 72
Urfa Kebabı / Fıstıklı Şiş Köfte
(Urfa Meatballs on Skewers / Pistachio Meatballs on Skewers) 70-71
Yoğurtlu Kebap (Kebap with Yoghurt) 80
Ezme (Spicy Tomato and Onion Salad) 38
Ezo Gelin Çorbası (Lentil and *Bulgur* Soup) 14

Fava (Broad Bean Purée) 28

Gavurdağı Salatası (Grilled Vegetable Salad) 31

Hamur İşleri (Pastry) 104-111
 Cevizli Erişte (Noodles with Cheese and Walnuts) 106
 Kabak Böreği (Courgette and Cheese Börek) 110
 Lahmacun (Savoury Flat Bread) 110-111
 Mantı (Meat Dumplings with Yoghurt) 107
 Saray Katmer (Spinach and Crèpes Gratin) 108
 Sigara Böreği (Rolls) 109
Haydari (Yoghurt and Cheese Spread) 37
Humus (Purée of Chickpeas) 32

Ilgaz Kebabı (*Ilgaz* Grilled Meat) 78
Ispanak Kökü Salatası (Spinach Root Salad) 30
Ispanaklı Yumurta (Eggs with Spinach) 42

İmam Bayıldı (Aubergines with Tomatoes and Onions) 50
İşkembe Çorbası (Tripe Soup) 20

Kabak Böreği (Courgette and Cheese Börek) 110
Kabak Dolması (Courgettes Stuffed with Meat) 58-59
Kabak Tatlısı (Pumpkin Pudding) 121
Kaburga (Grilled Ribs) 73
Kadınbudu Köfte (Lady's Thighs Meatball) 88
Kahve (Turkish Coffee) 130
Kaymaklı Kayısı Tatlısı (Dried Apricots Stuffed with Cream) 117
Kalamar Dolma (Stuffed Squid) 94
Kalkan Tava (Fried Turbot) 95
Karnıyarık (Aubergines Stuffed with Mincemeat) 60
Karides (Shrimps) 93
Keşkül (Almond Milk Pudding) 121
Kılıç Şiş (Swordfish on Skewers) 96
Kıymalı Pırasa (Leeks with Minced Meat) 66
Köfteler (Meatballs) 85-90
 Domates Soslu Köfte (Meatballs in Tomato Sauce) 89
 Kadınbudu Köfte (Lady's Thighs Meatball) 88
 Kuru Köfte (Fried Meatballs) 86
 Patates Köftesi (Potato Balls) 86
Kuru Fasulye (Bean Casserole) 67

Kuru Köfte (Fried Meatballs) 86
Lahmacun (Savoury Flat Bread) 110-111

Lüfer Izgara (Grilled Bluefish) 92

Mantı (Meat Dumplings with Yoghurt) 107
Meyhane Pilavı (Cracked Wheat (*Bulgur*) & Meat *Pilav*) 100
Meyva Hoşafı (Stewed Fruit) 126-127
Menemen (Eggs with Tomatoes and Green Peppers) 42
Mercimek Çorbası (Lentil Soup) 15
Mezeler (Mezes) 24-40
  Cacık (Yoghurt and Cucumber Salad) 26
  Çoban Salatası (Shepherd's Salad) 27
  Çerkez Tavuğu (Circassian Chicken) 28
  Ezme (Spicy Tomato and Onion Salad) 38
  Fava (Broad Beans Purée) 28
  Gavurdağı Salatası (Grilled Vegetable Salad) 31
  Humus (Purée of Chickpeas) 32
  Haydari (Yoghurt and Cheese Spread) 37
  Ispanak Kökü Salatası (Spinach Root Salad) 30
  Patates Salatası (Potato Salad) 33
  Patlıcan Salatası (Aubergine Purée) 36
  Sirkeli Patlıcan Salatası (Aubergine Salad with Vinegar) 36

Mısır Çorbası (Corn Soup) 13
Nohutlu Pilav (Rice with Chickpeas) 102

Pastırmalı Yumurta (Eggs with Pastırma) 45
Patates Salatası (Potato Salad) 33
Patates Köftesi (Potato Balls) 86
Patlıcan Salatası (Aubergine Purée) 36
Pilavlar (Rice Dishes) 98-103
  Meyhane Pilavı (Cracked Wheat (*Bulgur*) & Meat *Pilav*) 100
  Nohutlu Pilav (Rice with Chickpeas) 102
  Sebzeli Pilav (Rice with Vegetables) 100
  Sarı Pilav (Rice with Saffron) 103
Pirzola (Grilled Chops) 74

Rakı 132

Saray Katmer (Spinach and Crèpes Gratin) 108
Sarı Pilav (Rice with Saffron) 103
Sarmısaklı Yoğurtlu Patlıcan Salatası (Garlic Yoghurt Aubergine Salad/Purée) 36
Sebzeler (Vegetables) 56-67
  Etli Dolma (Vegetables Stuffed with Meat) 58
  Etli Bamya (Braised Meat with Okra) 61
  Etli Türlü (Meat Stew) 64
  Kabak Dolması (Courgettes Stuffed with Meat) 58-59

Kıymalı Pırasa (Leeks with Minced Meat) 66
Kuru Fasulye (Bean Casserole) 67
Karnıyarık (Aubergines Stuffed with Minced Meat) 60
Tavuklu Türlü (Chicken and Vegetable Stew) 62
Sigara Böreği (Rolls) 109
Sirkeli Patlıcan Salatası (Aubergine Salad with Vinegar) 36

Şiş Kebabı / Tavuk / Dana Eti Şiş
(Grilled Lamb on Skewers / Chicken / Veal) 74

Tatlılar (Dessert) 112-129
  Aşure (Noah's Pudding) 114
  Ayva Tatlısı (Quince Dessert) 116
  Kabak Tatlısı (Pumpkin Dessert) 120
  Kaymaklı Kayısı Tatlısı (Apricots Stuffed with Cream) 117
  Keşkül (Almond Milk Pudding) 120
  Meyva Hoşafı (Stewed Fruit) 126-127
  Vişne Kompostosu / Vişne Ekmek Tatlısı
  (Sour Cherry Compote / Sour Cherry Bread Pudding) 125
  Tarhana Çorbası (Winter Soup) 12
  Tavuklu Türlü (Chicken and Vegetable Stew) 62
  Tavuk Kanat Şiş (Grilled Chicken Wing on Skewers) 72

Urfa Kebabı / Fıstıklı Şiş Köfte
(Urfa Meatballs on Skewers / Pistachio Meatballs on Skewers) 70-71

Vişne Kompostosu / Vişne Ekmek Tatlısı
(Sour Cherry Compote / Sour Cherry Bread Pudding) 125

Yayla Çorbası (Yoghurt and Mint Soup) 16
Yumurtalar (Eggs) 41-45
  Çılbır (Egg with Yoghurt Sauce) 44
  Ispanaklı Yumurta (Eggs with Spinach) 42
  Menemen (Eggs with Tomatoes and Green Peppers) 42
  Pastırmalı Yumurta (Eggs with *Pastırma*) 45
Yoğurtlu Kebap (Kebap with Yoghurt) 80

Zeytinyağlı Yaprak / Lahana Dolması
(Stuffed Vine / Cabbage Leaves in Olive Oil) 52-53
Zeytinyağlı Pırasa (Leeks in Olive Oil) 54
Zeytinyağlı Taze Bakla (Fresh Broad Beans in Olive Oil) 55
Zeytinyağlılar (Olive Oil Dishes) 49-55
  İmam Bayıldı (Aubergines with Tomatoes and Onions) 50
  Zeytinyağlı Taze Fasulye (Green Beans in Olive Oil) 50-51
  Zeytinyağlı Pırasa (Leeks in Olive Oil) 54
  Zeytinyağlı Taze Bakla (Fresh Broad Beans in Olive Oil) 55
  Zeytinyağlı Taze Fasulye (Green Beans in Olive Oil) 50-51